2006

Biographies

Diego Rivera

Artist and Muralist

by Megan Schoeneberger

Consultant:
Curt Germundson, PhD
Art History Professor
Minnesota State University, Mankato
Mankato, Minnesota

Capstone
press

Mankato, Minnesota

Fact Finders is published by Capstone Press,
151 Good Counsel Drive, P.O. Box 669, Mankato, Minnesota 56002.
www.capstonepress.com

Library of Congress Cataloging-in-Publication Data
Schoeneberger, Megan.
    Diego Rivera: artist and muralist / by Megan Schoeneberger.
    p. cm.—(Fact finders. Biographies. Great Hispanics)
    Summary: "An introduction to the life of Diego Rivera, the Hispanic man who showed his love for art and Mexico through his numerous paintings and murals"—Provided by publisher.
    Includes bibliographical references and index.
    ISBN-13: 978-0-7368-5437-5 (hardcover)
    ISBN-10: 0-7368-5437-1 (hardcover)
    1. Rivera, Diego, 1886–1957—Juvenile literature. 2. Painters—Mexico—Biography—Juvenile literature. I. Rivera, Diego, 1886-1957. II. Title. III. Series.
ND259.R5S36 2006
759.972—dc22
                       2005021595

Editorial Credits
Amber Bannerman, editor; Juliette Peters, set designer; Linda Clavel and Scott Thoms, book designers;
    Wanda Winch, photo researcher/photo editor

Photo Credits
Bob Schalkwijk, 5, 8, 12, 18, 26; Bridgeman Art Library/Banco de Mexicano de Imagenes; INBA/Museo Dolores Olmedo Patino, Mexico City, Self Portrait, 1916 (oil on canvas), Rivera, Diego (1886–1957), 11; Bridgeman Art Library/Museo Nacional de Antropologia, Mexico City, Mexico, Banco Mexicano de Imagenes; INBA/Woman at the Well, 1913 (oil on canvas), Rivera, Diego (1886–1957), 13; Corbis/Bettmann, cover, 16; Corbis/Christie's Images, 14–15; Courtesy of Throckmorton Fine Art, New York, 24–25; Getty Images Inc./Hulton Archive, 17; Getty Images Inc./Time Life Pictures/Pix, Inc./Victor De Palma, 27; Globe Photos/Rangefinders, 1; Man at the Crossroads of Life, Unfinished Mural by Diego Rivera, Rockefeller Center, New York City, 1932, Photograph by Lucienne Bloch, 23; Peter A. Juley & Son Collection, Smithsonian American Art Museum, Smithsonian Institution, 21; Photo courtesy of the Fundacion Diego Rivera A.C., Mexico City, 7, 9, 19; Rivera painting, "Infant in the Bulb of a Plant," Courtesy of the Rivera Archives, Photograph, 1932, The Detroit Institute of Arts, 22

Permission to reproduce works of art by Diego Rivera for pages 8, 11, 13, 15, 18, 22, 23, and 25 is granted by 2005 Banco de Mexico Diego Rivera & Frida Kahlo Museums Trust, Ave. Cinco de Mayo No. 2, Col. Centro, Del. Cuauhtemoc 06059, Mexico D.F. Permission to reproduce works of art by Diego Rivera for pages 11, 13, 15, 18, 23, and 25 is also granted by el Instituto Nacional de Bellas Artes y Literatura (INBA).

1 2 3 4 5 6 11 10 09 08 07 06

Table of Contents

Chapter 1

Studying Cézanne

Diego Rivera stood as still as a statue outside an art **gallery** in Paris, France. He had been staring in the window for hours. Rivera had come to Paris in the spring of 1909. He was there to study art.

A painting by Paul Cézanne, Rivera's favorite artist, hung in the window. Rivera was amazed. He stared, trying to learn every color and brush stroke. The dealer brought more Cézanne paintings to the window. Rivera studied each one.

Night fell. Rain began to fall. Still, Rivera waited for more paintings. Finally, the dealer told Rivera to go home. He had no more Cézannes to show him.

Diego Rivera used this passport photograph when he traveled to different countries.

Soaked, Rivera went home and dreamed of painting like Cézanne. But instead of hanging in galleries, Rivera's paintings would be out in the open. Everybody, rich and poor, would see his **murals**.

Chapter 2

Childhood

On December 8, 1886, Diego Rivera and his twin brother, Carlos, were born in Guanajuato, Mexico. Their parents, Diego and María Rivera, did not expect twins. Diego was the older twin. His brother was small and weak. When the twins were less than 2 years old, Carlos became ill and died.

When Rivera turned 2, he was thin and sickly. His parents sent him to a nurse, Antonia. She took him to her home in the mountains. There, he played in the fresh air and sunlight. He grew strong.

Two years later, Rivera returned to Guanajuato to live with his parents. His sister, María, was born when he was 5 years old.

Carlos (left) and Diego (right) pose for a picture at age 1.

A Young Artist

As soon as he could hold a pencil, Rivera began to draw. He drew trains and battle scenes. His drawings covered the walls, the doors, and the furniture of his home. Finally, Rivera's father set aside a room just for the little boy. He covered the walls and floors with canvas. There, Rivera could draw as much as he wanted without ruining the family's things.

FACT!

As a young boy, Rivera dreamed of becoming an engineer. He spent hours at the train station, watching the trains come and go.

Rivera drew this detailed picture with a pencil when he was a young boy. ▼

Rivera (back row, second from right) sits with his classmates in 1902 at the San Carlos School of Fine Arts.

School

When Rivera was 6, his family moved to Mexico City. The next year, Rivera began school. At age 9, Rivera began going to night classes at the San Carlos School of Fine Arts. At age 12, he became a full-time student there. While there, Rivera learned how to show distance in his paintings. He also learned about Mexican art from long ago. In this art, Rivera saw joy, hope, and fear.

Chapter 3

Studying in Europe

Rivera finished the art school in 1906, at age 20. Soon after, he met a Mexican painter known as Dr. Atl, who had just returned from Europe. Rivera decided to travel to Madrid, Spain, to study with Atl's friend Eduardo Chicharro.

When Rivera reached Spain in January of 1907, he set up his easel and began painting in Chicharro's studio. He worked with Chicharro from dawn until past midnight most days.

Two years later, Rivera moved to Paris, France. He spent his days in art museums, painting along the Seine River, and searching art galleries for paintings by his favorite artists. But he missed Mexico.

Rivera painted this picture of himself while he was studying in Europe.

▲ Angelina Beloff met Rivera in Paris in 1911.

A Visit Home

In 1910, Rivera went back to Mexico to show his paintings. His show opened on November 20 and lasted for one month. Thirteen of his 35 paintings were sold.

While in Mexico, Rivera noticed the red, brown, and green colors of the land. His homeland inspired his paintings. He soon began painting scenes of Mexico's countryside.

Rivera returned to Europe in 1911. While there, he met Russian painter Angelina Beloff. The two became close.

A New Style

In 1913, Rivera tried a new style of art called **cubism**. In this style, painters tried to show several points of view at one time. He became friends with the leading cubist painter of the time, Pablo Picasso.

In 1916, Beloff and Rivera had a son together. They named him Diego. He died 14 months later.

Rivera's 1913 oil on canvas called *Woman at the Well* is similar in style to Pablo Picasso's paintings.

QUOTE

"Cubism broke down forms as they had been seen for centuries and was creating out of the fragments new forms . . . new worlds."
—Diego Rivera

13

Chapter 4

Art for the People

In 1920, Rivera traveled to Italy. There, he saw huge paintings on ceilings in churches and other public buildings. Anyone could view these masterpieces without having to pay. Rivera wanted art to be free and open to everyone. By painting on walls of public buildings, he could bring art to the people.

For years, critics had praised Rivera's cubist paintings. But Rivera soon realized that he needed to move on from cubism. He wanted to paint what he knew and loved. For Rivera, that meant painting about Mexico. He combined what he knew about European art with what he knew about ancient Mexican art. Rivera started to find his own style.

Rivera's *Flower Vendor* showed the beauty of Mexico's workers.

People gather in Mexico in the Plaza at Tampico during the Mexican Revolution.

Back to Mexico

Rivera returned to Mexico in 1921. He left Beloff behind, and never returned for her. Mexico had changed since Rivera's last visit. In 1910, a **revolution** had begun. Mexicans were upset with President Porfirio Díaz. Under Díaz, workers' wages were low. Workers rose up against Díaz. Throughout the fighting, Mexico's leaders changed several times.

When Rivera arrived in Mexico, Álvaro Obregón had just become Mexico's president. The new government wanted to educate the people about their Mexican **identity**. They hired artists to paint murals on public buildings, where all people could see them. The murals would celebrate Mexico's culture and show the story of its past. The minister of education, José Vasconcelos, was in charge of the project.

FACT!

Álvaro Obregón was reelected for Mexican presidency in 1928, but was assasinated before he could take office.

Álvaro Obregón was Mexico's president from 1920 to 1924. ▼

17

Rivera's Murals

In 1921, Vasconcelos hired Rivera to paint a wall at the National Preparatory School. Rivera began work the following year. It took about 15 months to plan and paint his first mural.

While working on the mural, Rivera met Guadalupe Marin, who modeled for him. In June 1922, they married. They later had two daughters, Lupe and Ruth.

Some of the figures in Rivera's *Creation* mural are over 12 feet (3.7 meters) tall. ▼

Rivera stands with his two daughters Lupe (left) and Ruth (right) in 1952.

In 1923, Rivera began painting murals in the Ministry of Education building. There, his murals focused on the lives of Mexican workers and farmers. They also showed Mexican celebrations and folk songs.

For the next few years, he continued to work on more murals for the Mexican government. With every painting, he celebrated the beauty and strength of ordinary Mexican people.

Chapter 5

Growing Fame

In 1927, Rivera separated from his wife, Guadalupe. He soon met a young artist named Frida Kahlo. The two were married in 1929. Rivera was 43, while Kahlo was only 23.

Rivera's mural at the Ministry of Education made him famous throughout the world. He began to travel to paint murals and show his work. In 1931, he was paid $1,500 to paint a mural at the California Fine Arts School in San Francisco. The New York Museum of Modern Art showed 150 of his paintings in 1931. The show broke attendance records at the museum.

Despite their age difference,
Rivera and Frida Kahlo became close.

A Mural for Hope

In 1932, Rivera went to Detroit, Michigan. There, he painted a mural on the walls of the Detroit Institute of Arts. Rivera's painting honored American workers. At the time, the United States was in the middle of the Great Depression (1929–1939). Many people had lost jobs. The mural showed workers as heroes and gave them hope.

A Huge Disagreement

In 1933, Rivera traveled to New York City to paint a mural in Rockefeller Center. Rivera included a picture of Russian **communist** leader Vladimir Lenin in the mural. Nelson Rockefeller became upset because he didn't agree with Lenin's ideas. He told Rivera to remove Lenin's picture. Rivera refused. Rockefeller had the mural destroyed.

Rivera's *Man at the Crossroads* mural showing Vladimir Lenin (right side; with mustache and beard) was chipped away from the wall and eventually destroyed. ▼

Chapter 6

Final Years

Rivera returned to Mexico City in 1934, to work on his murals in the National Palace. For the next several years, Rivera divided his attention between his paintings and his wife. A childhood accident had left Kahlo in constant pain. When Rivera wasn't painting, he helped care for her. Rivera and Kahlo did not always get along. In 1939, they divorced. But one year later, they remarried.

On July 13, 1954, Kahlo died. In early 1955, Rivera was diagnosed with cancer. That September, he suffered a blood clot that left him unable to move his right arm. He still tried to paint as often as he could. On November 24, 1957, Rivera's heart failed. He died at the age of 70.

Kahlo watches Rivera paint at the National Palace.

▲ Rivera's love for painting shines through his smile while he paints in his studio in Mexico City.

QUOTE

"An artist is above all a human being . . . if the artist isn't capable of loving until he forgets himself . . . then he isn't a great artist."

—Diego Rivera

Rivera's Legacy

Rivera's murals changed Americans' ideas of public art. Following the Great Depression, President Franklin Delano Roosevelt started a program for American murals. His program gave work to more than 5,000 artists.

Throughout his life, Rivera believed that art could change the world. He used his art to change the way Mexicans saw themselves. His murals also changed the way people from other countries saw Mexico. Today, when people think of Mexico, they think of the bright colors in Rivera's paintings.

Fast Facts

Full name: Diego Rivera
Birth: December 8, 1886
Death: November 24, 1957
Hometown: Guanajuato, Mexico
Parents: Diego and María Rivera
Wives: Guadalupe Marin (1922–1927); Frida Kahlo (1929–1939; 1940–1954)
Children: son, Diego; daughters, Lupe and Ruth
Education: San Carlos School of Fine Arts, 1895–1906
Major Paintings:

> *Creation*, National Preparatory School, Mexico City, 1922–1923
>
> *Labours and Festivals of the Mexican People and The Mexican Revolution*, Ministry of Education, Mexico City, 1923–1928
>
> *History of Mexico*, Staircase of the National Palace, Mexico City, 1929–1935
>
> *The Making of a Fresco*, San Francisco Art Institute, San Francisco, California, 1931
>
> *Detroit Industry*, The Detroit Institute of Arts, Detroit, Michigan, 1932–1933
>
> *Prehispanic and Colonial Mexico*, Corridor of the National Palace, Mexico City, 1942–1951

Time Line

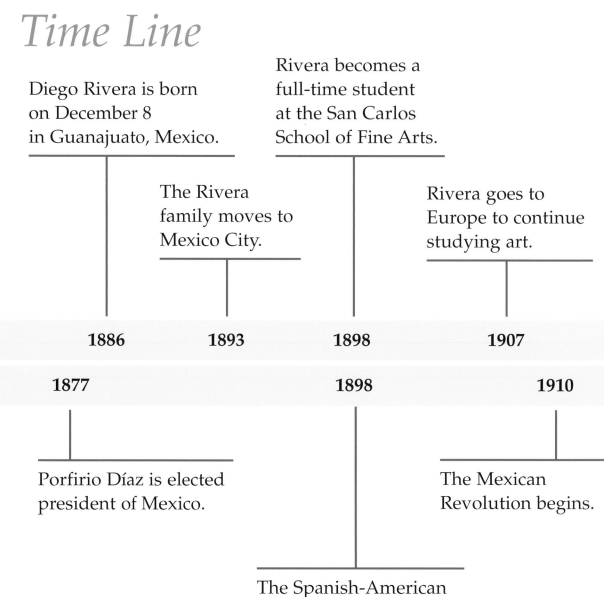

Life Events of Diego Rivera

Diego Rivera is born on December 8 in Guanajuato, Mexico.

Rivera becomes a full-time student at the San Carlos School of Fine Arts.

The Rivera family moves to Mexico City.

Rivera goes to Europe to continue studying art.

| 1886 | 1893 | 1898 | 1907 |

| 1877 | | 1898 | 1910 |

Events in History

Porfirio Díaz is elected president of Mexico.

The Mexican Revolution begins.

The Spanish-American War is fought.

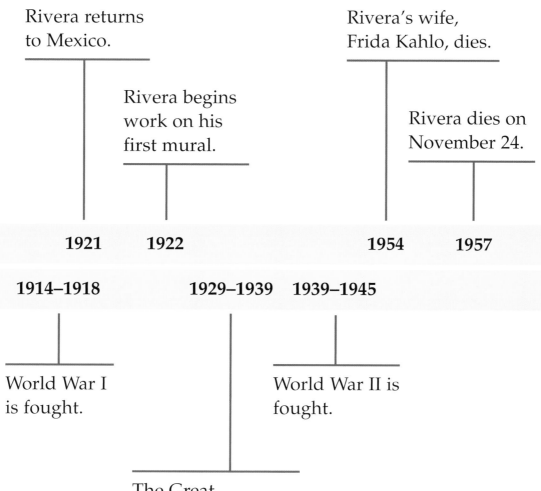

Rivera returns
to Mexico.

Rivera's wife,
Frida Kahlo, dies.

Rivera begins
work on his
first mural.

Rivera dies on
November 24.

1921　　**1922**　　　　　　**1954**　　**1957**

1914–1918　　　　**1929–1939**　**1939–1945**

World War I
is fought.

World War II is
fought.

The Great
Depression occurs.

Glossary

communist (KOM-yuh-nist)—having to do with supporting communism; communism is a way of organizing a country so that all the land, houses, and factories belong to the government or community as a whole.

cubism (KYOOB-iz-uhm)—an art style in which artists break objects, people, and landscapes into simple shapes

gallery (GAL-uh-ree)—a place where paintings, sculptures, photographs, and other types of art are displayed and sometimes sold

identity (eye-DEN-ti-tee)—who a person or group is

mural (MYU-ruhl)—a large work of art on a wall or a ceiling

revolution (rev-uh-LOO-shuhn)—an uprising by people who try to change their country's system of government

Internet Sites

FactHound offers a safe, fun way to find Internet sites related to this book. All of the sites on FactHound have been researched by our staff.

Here's how:

1. Visit *www.facthound.com*
2. Type in this special code **0736854371** for age-appropriate sites. Or enter a search word related to this book for a more general search.
3. Click on the **Fetch It** button.

FactHound will fetch the best sites for you!

Read More

Bankston, John. *Diego Rivera.* Latinos in American History. Hockessin, Del.: Mitchell Lane Publishers, 2004.

Carew-Miller, Anna. *Mexican Art and Architecture.* Mexico, Our Southern Neighbor. Philadelphia: Mason Crest Publishers, 2003.

Litwin, Laura Baskes. *Diego Rivera: Legendary Mexican Painter.* Latino Biography Library. Berkeley Heights, N.J.: Enslow, 2005.

Index